The Ultimate
MINISTRY TOOL BOX SERIES

How to
Write a Book

Daniel King

How to Write a Book

ISBN: 1-931810-13-3

Copyright: 2010
Daniel King
King Ministries International
PO Box 701113
Tulsa, OK 74170 USA
1-877-431-4276
daniel@kingministries.com
www.kingministries.com

Table of Contents

Have you ever read a book that made an eternal impact on your life?

Introduction

Have you ever read a book that made an eternal impact on your life? Can you think of a particular author who totally revolutionized your thinking when you read his book? Perhaps you were in need of an answer, a solution, insight, or wisdom, and you found it while perusing the pages of a deeply thought-provoking book. Maybe you've come across a book whose message so strongly stirred your heart that you thought if no one else ever read it, that book was written just for you.

The written word is a timeless vehicle of power and change. Books can outlive their authors, and the message contained within their pages can be passed down from one generation to the next. Just think of all the ancient books that have shaped your thinking, transformed your life, or strengthened your faith. Where would you be without those books? Furthermore, where would you be without the writers who dared to apply pen to paper, heart to page, and message to print? We owe much of who we are to those men and women who boldly preserved on the printed page the message God placed in their hearts.

Several years ago, I was in the nation of Congo in the heart of Africa. I was preaching in a small hut that was jammed full of over 200 people. Chickens ran across the dirt floor as the congregation enthusiastically praised the Lord. I glanced over at the young pastor and noticed he was holding his Bible and another dog-eared book that was carefully covered in duct tape.

"Show me what you are reading," I asked him. When he handed me the book, I recognized the cover. It was written by my friend and mentor, the great missionary evangelist T.L. Osborn.

I asked, "Where did you get this book?"

He explained, "Twenty years ago, Dr. Osborn came to my nation. My father got saved at his meeting and decided to become a pastor. Dr. Osborn gave him this book and for twenty years my father preached sermons from this book. Last year my father died and I became the pastor of this church. Now I preach from the same book."

When I heard the pastor's story, I realized the impact one book could have. T.L. Osborn's books have impacted the world, and because of his example, I started to write. I trust the message God has given me will reach farther and faster because I took the time to preserve it on the printed page.

If God has given you a message that is burning in your heart, I challenge you to begin writing it down for others to read. Your words can make a difference in the lives of others, bringing peace, hope, salvation, and healing to a broken and dying world. As a minister, you have been given the responsibility of carrying the message of the Gospel; as a writer, you can excel in your mission by preserving that message for generations to come.

Chapter 1

Why Should You Write a Book?

Because books have a durable quality, they are worth the investment of time and money it takes to write one. In terms of cost and profit, a published book containing the powerful truth of the Gospel has infinite rewards. Here are several reasons why you should write a book.

1. Books help believers grow spiritually. One of the challenges of every evangelist is to turn converts into disciples. How can a new believer grow from saying a salvation prayer into a strong follower of Jesus? I believe one key to solving this problem is putting a book in the hands of the new believer. God did not call me specifically to be an author; God called me to be an evangelist, and I discovered that writing books helps me be a better evangelist.

2. Books continue to preach the Gospel long after you return home. Books can go farther than I can go, stay longer than I can stay, and impact lives I can never reach. By writing books, I am imitating God. A book can go where you cannot go and speak where you cannot speak. Our heavenly Father sent his Son for a season, but He left His Book forever.

3. Books are often shared and read by many different family members and neighbors. After one of our festivals, we did a survey and discovered an amazing fact. Each book that we gave

away was read by an average of ten people. So, if we give away ten thousand books, we can potentially impact over one hundred thousand people. A book is a seed that keeps producing all over the world.

4. Books are treasured by new believers. In all our festivals, I have never seen one of our books thrown to the ground and trampled underfoot. Each one is valued and read. Recently a woman named Maria gave her life to Jesus during one of our great Gospel festivals. After a counselor handed her a book, tears poured from her eyes as she said, "Thank you!" I saw her reading the book as she walked toward her bus. She would take a step and read a page, then take another step. I am sure she read the entire book before she ever arrived home.

5. Books are more durable than the spoken word. The written word is more permanent than the spoken word. Cassette tapes, videos, and DVDs are rarely listened to more than once, but a well-loved book is taken off the shelf and referred to repeatedly. A book is simply more credible, more believable, and more enduring than other mediums of communication.

6. Books help you spread your message. Recognize the value of a book. If God has given you a message for mankind, you should share it by writing a book. If your message is worth preaching, it is worth putting in a book. If you are preaching something that is not worth putting in a book, why are you preaching it? If it is worth putting in a book, it is worth giving that book away to thousands.

7. A book is your lasting legacy. Robb Thompson said, "The only thing you'll ever leave in this life are your books. If you

leave money, someone will spend it." At the end of the 1800's there were two well-known churches in London. The first was called City Temple pastored by Joseph Parker. The other church was known as Metropolitan Tabernacle led by Charles Spurgeon. In their own time, both pastors had large congregations and were equally famous. But today no one knows who Parker was, but every preacher has heard of Spurgeon because of the lasting impact of his books. A book creates an enduring legacy that will live on longer than you.

*The only tool
we have
to work with
is words.*

Chapter 2

God Wants You to Write

God is Spirit. He is not physically present here on earth. We cannot touch Him or feel Him, but we can hear His words. When God wants to accomplish something, He uses His words. When God created light, He said, "Let there be light." When God wanted to save the world, He sent His Son, known as "The Word." God moves on this earth through His words. God is a writer. The Bible is a collection of God's words.

We are the same as God. The only tool we have to work with is words. Words are what change people's hearts. Our words decide what others feel, think, and do. We cannot physically force anyone to do our will; we can only convince them with our words. Our words are powerful, both in spoken form and in written form. Books allow us to use words, our greatest weapon.

The servants of God are commanded to write. Moses (Exodus 17:14), Nehemiah (Nehemiah 9:38), Isaiah (Isaiah 30:8), Jeremiah (Jeremiah 30:2), Ezekiel (Ezekiel 43:11), and the Apostle James (Acts 15:20) all obeyed the command to write. We should also obey God's divine command to document our spiritual discoveries.

Here are a few instructions to consider when you begin writing:

1. Write to record God's instructions. Deuteronomy 27:8 says, *"And you shall write very plainly on the stones all the words of this law."*

2. Write what God tells you. Isaiah 8:1 states, *"The Lord said to me, 'Take a large scroll, and write on it with a man's pen...'"*

3. Write about your vision and your calling. Habakkuk 2:2 says, *"Write the vision and make it plain on tablets, That he may run who reads it."*

4. Write what you know about Jesus. Luke recorded the following in his Gospel: *"Inasmuch as many have taken in hand to set in order a narrative of those things which have been fulfilled among us, just as those who from the beginning were eyewitnesses and ministers of the word delivered them to us, it seemed good to me also, having had perfect understanding of all things from the very first, to write to you an orderly account, most excellent Theophilus, that you may know the certainty of those things in which you were instructed"* (Luke 1:1-4).

5. Write to warn of sin. Paul wrote to the church at Corinth: *"I do not write these things to shame you, but as my beloved children I warn you"* (1 Corinthians 4:14).

6. Write to instruct your spiritual sons. Paul wrote to Timothy: *"I write so that you may know how you ought to conduct yourself in the house of God"* (1 Timothy 3:15).

7. Write to encourage people in the Lord. In his epistle, John recorded: *"And these things we write to you that your joy may be full"* (1 John 1:4).

8. Write about living a life of faith. Jude 1:3 says, *"Beloved, while I was very diligent to write to you concerning our common salvation, I found it necessary to write to you exhorting you to contend earnestly for the faith which was once for all delivered to the saints."*

*Getting started
is the most
challenging stage
in the
writing process.*

Chapter 3

Start Your Book

Most everyone will agree that getting started is the most challenging stage in the writing process. First paragraphs, first thoughts, and first sentences are almost never the final ones that appear in your published manuscript. As you begin the writing process, it's important to remain patient while maintaining vigilance and focus. Your dedication will pay off in the end.

As you sit down with paper and pen in hand, think about your writing goals. Why are you writing, what are you writing about, and who is your audience? While you're tapping out words on your laptop, write to document your persuasions, your discoveries, your beliefs, and your greatest ideas. Write to influence, to inform, and to persuade.

While you're brainstorming your first book, I have a few suggestions to help get the creative juices flowing. Take a piece of paper and answer the questions listed below. Your answers will show what topics you should focus on as you write.

* What is important to you?

* What do you think about?

* What do you talk about the most?

* What challenges have you overcome in life?

* What problems have you solved?

* What topics do you know well?

* What is God speaking to you about?

Are you excited about children, restoration, faith, love, music, or marriage? What subject do you think about the most? Every minister should write a book on his primary focus. For example, my passion is soulwinning. Because of this passion, I have written several books about soulwinning including *Soulwinning: Inspiration for Winning the Lost, You can Become a Master Soulwinner*, and *The Call of the Soulwinner*.

If you could talk to anybody about one thing, what would it be? If you have five minutes left on the earth and you could speak about one thing, what would that subject be? This topic that you are passionate about is what you should write about.

On the line below, write one word that expresses what you are most passionate about: _____

Below, write down seven facts you know about this subject, seven things you believe, and seven truths you have discovered about your favorite subject. Use these seven facts as the foundation for the chapters in your book.

1. _____

2. _____

3. _____

4. _____

5. _____

6. _____

7. _____

Acclaimed author Jim Stoval once told me there are three elements to every book. First, there is information. What do you know? Second, there is story. How do you know what you know? How did you discover the truth you know? Third, there is humor and emotion. What moment did you discover what you know? Is there a humorous story about the mistakes you made before you learned what you know? Or is your story tragic?

Below, write down seven experiences in your life that relate to your topic.

1. _____

2. _____

3. _____

4. _____

5. _____

6. _____

7. _____

What are seven scriptures that relate to your subject?

1. _____

2. _____

3. _____

4. _____

5. _____

6. _____

7. _____

* Use the ideas you have written down to write an outline for your book. What will your Table of Contents look like?

* At the beginning of your book, identify a problem and use it to grab the reader's attention. What need are you addressing? What is your solution? Explain to your reader the specific steps he can take to apply the solution to his life.

* In the introduction to your book, explain your unique life experience that gives you the credentials to write about your subject. What pain have you experienced? What discoveries have you made along life's journey? What did you go through that qualifies you to write?

* Do not fill the beginning of your book with boring background material. Spread this throughout your book so the reader continues to read.

* At the end of your book, conclude on an encouraging note. Challenge your readers to take action. Give your reader something to think about, something he can use in his life.

Chapter 4

Keys to Writing Your Book

Writing a book is not an easy process; it requires determination, creativity, and focus. The more you polish your writing skills, the better you will become as an author. Here are a few keys to help guide you in crafting your book.

1. Develop your information system. I have identified over 100 subjects that I want to write on in my lifetime. I have a file on my computer for each of these subjects. When God speaks to me about leadership, I type the thought into my file on leadership. When my wife and I have a great time on a date, I record my impressions for my future book on marriage. When I am reading my Bible and a verse leaps out at me about sowing seed, I record the reference in a document about giving and receiving. When I listen to a sermon about King David, I take notes and drop them into my file on the life of King David. Later, when I have time to write a book about each of these subjects, I will already have a lifetime of notes from which to draw. Developing a systematic filing system for recording good ideas and one-liners is key to keeping track of your thoughts and impressions as you prepare to write a book.

2. Record your discoveries about God's Word. For many years, I documented my discoveries about God in the margins of my Bible. One day as I was returning home from a mission trip, my Bible was inside a suitcase that was lost by the airline. My heart

sank. Years of study were lost in a moment. For three days I was horribly disappointed, but then I received a call. The airline had found my bag. When my Bible was back in my hands, I held it close to my chest and kissed the cover. I was so happy to recover my lost revelations. I vowed that I would never lose them again. I spent days going through God's Word and typing up all my notes. Now I have a document on my computer that contains my thoughts about every book in the Bible. Eventually, these ideas will become sermons and books that will impact thousands of lives.

3. Use a digital voice recorder. You can speak ten times faster then you can write. A digital voice recorder can capture your thoughts, ideas, and God's instructions. Your mind is better used for creativity than storage. Once you record your ideas, have them transcribed.

4. Keep a notebook beside your bed when you go to sleep. Keep another one in your secret place where you go to pray. As a wise sage said, "A short pencil is better than a long memory."

5. Identify who your main reader is. Who will benefit from your book? Put a picture in front of you of the person for whom you are writing. Write as if you are speaking to that person throughout your manuscript. It is important to capture the attention of your reader. Seven out of ten books that are purchased are not read. Only one out of ten books are read past the first chapter.

6. Identify the best time for you to write. When do you feel the most creative? Early in the morning? Right before you go to bed? At a coffee shop? When lots of people are around? Do you like to write as you listen to worship music, or do you prefer the at-

mosphere to be absolutely quiet? Each person is different. Find out where and when you do your best work.

7. Write every day. Make a daily habit of writing. Do not set your initial goals too high. Open your laptop or notebook and force yourself to write 500-1000 words every day. Start by writing the first paragraph and then work on the second. Set a small, achievable goal each day and accomplish it. Daily discipline will eventually produce results. I make it a goal to write on a daily basis. Some days I type just a few words; other days I write several thousand words.

8. Set a deadline to finish your book. A goal is a vision with a deadline attached. Deadlines create motivation and a sense of urgency.

9. Recognize that writing can be hard work. Like any activity worth doing, writing is not a skill you become an expert at overnight. Your initial idea for your book is probably brilliant, but like a diamond in the rough, it is revealed by cutting away unnecessary material and a long process of polishing.

You will need to hone your skills, rewrite your material, edit your words, and polish your work until it is perfect. This requires patience and tenacity, so don't give up when you become discouraged.

I worked every day for one year on my first book. At the end of the year, I read through everything I had written and discovered that it was not a well-written book. It was full of Christian clichés, generalities, and random scriptures that had nothing to do with the subject on which I was writing. I threw out the first three chapters and the final three chapters and used the middle of the book as the foundation for my first published work, *Fire Power*.

Winston Churchill once said, "Writing a book is an adventure. To begin with, it is a toy and an amusement. Then it becomes a mistress, then it becomes a master, then it becomes a tyrant. The last phase is that just as you are about to become reconciled to your servitude, you kill the monster and fling him about to the public."

10. Study what others have written. I met a young man who wanted to write a book on the fire of God. I handed him a copy of my book *Fire Power* that talks about how to catch the fire of God, keep the fire of God, and spread the fire of God. He declined to read my book because he felt he already knew everything there was to know about the subject. No matter how much he thought he already knew about the fire of God, he could have gleaned something new from reading others' writings on this topic.

Before I wrote my book *Healing Power*, I read over 250 books on the subject of healing. Some of the books said that God does not heal today; others were written by the greatest healing evangelists in history. Everything I read helped me write a better book. If you write before studying, your opinion will be uninformed.

Look at what other people are writing on your chosen subject. How is your book different? What does your book contribute? What can you say that no one else has ever said? How will your story help people understand the subject in a new way?

11. Write simply enough that a third-grader can understand. You do not need to impress people with your use of weird, archaic terminology. Write to communicate, not to confuse.

12. Read your writing aloud to discover how it sounds.

13. Set aside your manuscript for a month and then come back to it. When you return you will have a fresh perspective.

14. Write to help the reader. Many novice authors make the mistake of writing what they want to write instead of writing what will help the reader. Always keep your reader in mind. The most important question any author can ask himself is: How will this help my reader?

15. Use personal stories to keep your readers interested. People love to know more about you. The more personal your writing, the more people will be able to relate to you. Often I skip the teaching parts of books I'm reading and head straight for the stories.

If you are sharing true stories, keep the confidentiality of real people in mind. If you do not have their permission to share the story, you must change the details so they cannot be recognized. Don't lie or make up details about stories.

Be creative first and edit later.

Chapter 5

Edit Your Book

Because writing and editing are two separate activities, don't create and edit at the same time. Be creative first and edit later. When you start the writing process, don't worry about your writing being perfect. Let ideas flow out of you uninterrupted. Later, go back and use the editing process to make revisions and polish your writing. Below are listed several steps to help you with the editing process of your book.

1. Be clear.

2. Stick to your topic.

3. Avoid repetition and redundancy and repetition.

4. Use strong language; be precise. Use action verbs, not passive verbs.

5. What you remove is just as important as what you leave in. Eliminate everything that does not belong there. As a writer, I tend to fall in love with my own words. After I am finished writing, I have to go back and get rid of all the bunny trails. One professor of writing said, "Omit needless words! Vigorous writing is concise! A sentence should contain no unnecessary words, and a paragraph should have no unnecessary sentences for the same reason that a drawing should have no unnecessary lines and a machine no unnecessary parts!" If in doubt, leave it out.

6. Check every sentence, paragraph, and chapter. Make sure they flow together in a logical manner. Each paragraph should only communicate one idea.

7. Express your opinions as opinions, not as facts.

8. Check your quotes and facts for accuracy.

9. Do not plagiarize. Cite original sources for the words and ideas of others.

10. Remove "Christianese" jargon. Will your reader know what "washed in the blood of the Lamb" means? What does "carry your cross daily" convey to a reader who is not a believer? Why do we say "give your heart to Jesus"?

Chapter 6

Design
Your Book

Now that your book is written, what do you need to do before you print your book? Although you may have the greatest message in the world, you still need professional critique on the content, and an attractive design to package your message. Here are a few tips to help you package the inside and outside of your book with creativity and excellence.

Design the interior of your book

1. Set the margins in Microsoft Word to book size so you can visualize your book as you write. The typical book is 5.25 inches by 8.25 inches. Set your margins to 1 inch at the top, bottom, and sides.

2. Make your book easy to read. Do not use any wild or hard-to-read fonts.

3. Put a page number on every page.

4. Hire a professional to layout your book for you.

5. Write short chapters. In the past, chapters were long. Now, with the advent of the Internet, people have much shorter attention spans. Few people have time or the patience to read a long chapter. Make your chapters short; you may even want to start a new chapter

every two pages. The goal of your book is to get people to read it, not to bore people with long chapters.

Hire an editor

Put together a team to help you complete your book. Because your writing will always sound brilliant to your own ears, it is important to have another person critique your book before you publish. Even if you are a good writer, a professional editor will help take your "good" manuscript and transform it into a piece of excellence.

A qualified editor will identify unclear areas, help you reorganize your thinking, or add explanatory text where needed. Professional editors are not only trained to clarify thought flow and correct grammar, but they are also familiar with the standards used in the publishing industry. Apart from enhancing your manuscript with quality grammar and literary style, editors will also help you maintain excellence matching industry standards.

Ask a proofreader to correct your book

Begin by asking friends and family members to proofread your book. They will catch some of your mistakes. However, I also highly recommend using a professional proofreader. Give your proofreader your final typeset manuscript. A good proofreader will check for spelling mistakes, grammatical errors, punctuation problems, accuracy in the text, lack of consistency in the layout, improper usage of bold and italics, and check for accurate quotation of Bible verses. However, usually the proofreader does not rewrite or change your writing style. By having a good proofreader, you will avoid embarrassing mistakes and costly reprints.

Design your book cover

Recently, a minister handed me his book. The cover was black and white with an ugly picture. It was obvious he had spent no money on the cover. I have no idea if the book was worth reading. Since the cover was ugly, I never even opened the book. Harsh? Yes, but this is what most readers do.

People say, "Don't judge a book by its cover," but the truth is that everyone does. If your cover looks cheap, then people will automatically assume you have nothing valuable to say. If you truly believe in your message, then invest in the look of your book. Spend the money to make the cover of your book attractive so that people will want to read it. Since the cover is the single most important part of your book, this is not the place to cut corners.

Tips for the cover:

1. Go to a bookstore and examine a variety of book covers. Pick your favorite look and take it to your designer and ask him to imitate the cover. Don't copy it exactly, but by using similar fonts and colors, you will end up with a professional-looking book.

2. Put the price on the back.

3. Put your picture on the cover of the book. You are selling more than just the subject of your book; you are really selling yourself and your understanding of the subject. Many people buy books because they like the author.

4. Put your contact information on the back of the book and inside the front cover. Your book is a like a large business card, except that people hardly ever throw away a book. It would be a big

mistake for someone to want to purchase hundreds of copies of your book and be unable to contact you.

Choose a title for your book

The title (and subtitle) of your book definitely helps sell your work. Your title should attract the reader's attention and inspire him to read the book. Often authors wait to title the work until after they have finished the book. They look for an image, quote, or idea from their writing that communicates the main idea of their book. That perfect title is somewhere within your book's contents.

My best-selling book is *The Secret of Obed-Edom*. It took me two years to write the book, and for a long-time I planned to title it *The Blessing of Obed-Edom*. But right before I published it, I found that someone else had already used this title for a sermon. I could have still used my original title because legally you cannot copyright the title of a work; however, I did not want to cause confusion when I started to market the book. I also knew people would be intrigued to discover what the "secret" is.

Then I started working on the subtitle. Since hardly anyone has ever heard of the Biblical character of Obed-Edom, I knew the subtitle would be an extremely important part of selling the book. I listed every word I could think of that would communicate the main thrust of the book. I wanted my subtitle to also connect the teaching to the reader's life. After exploring hundreds of possible words, I finally decided to subtitle the book "An ancient story with hidden truth for your spiritual journey." Often while talking about Obed-Edom, I call the book, "The greatest undiscovered story in the Bible."

If you get stuck trying to think of a captivating subtitle, ask some creative individuals to help you. For example, the subtitle for my book *Fire Power: Igniting Genuine Passion for Jesus* was suggested by John Mason, an author who has a brilliant way with words. Chances are someone you know will be able to create a catchy phrase to describe the book's message.

Use your title to create curiosity and catch people's attention. Use your subtitle to add more explanation and to convince the reader that he or she cannot live without your book. A great selling book will have both an excellent title and an informative subtitle.

Ask for endorsements

During my final year of college at Oral Roberts University, the theology department gave me the Senior Paper of the Year Award for my paper on healing. I had the opportunity to meet the Board of Regents including Marilyn Hickey, the chairperson of the board. I spoke to her for less than thirty seconds, and she asked me to mail her a copy of my paper. When I did, I told her I was writing a book on healing and asked if she would be willing to write the foreword for my book. To my delight, she agreed.

Her endorsement of my book gave me instant credibility. People had never heard of me, but they knew her. Many people bought my book because of her recommendation.

Ask well-known ministers to endorse your book. Send them a brief letter asking for a short endorsement. Ask your pastor to write your foreword. If you have a mentor, ask him to recommend your work. Include these endorsements on the back cover of your book.

Now that your book is written, edited, proofread, and designed, it's time to send it to press!

Chapter 7

Publish Your Book

Now that your book is written, edited, proofread, and designed, it's time to send it to press! With today's technology, there are a variety of ways to publish your book. Below I have listed the main avenues for publishing your manuscript.

1. Traditional Publisher. The traditional idea most people have in their minds of publishing is for a publisher to give an author a cash advance, spend thousands of dollars marketing the book, and then send the author huge royalty checks. Unfortunately, it is extremely hard to find a publisher who is willing to publish a first-time author.

If you do want to go this route, try hiring a literary agent. Or, try researching which publishers are printing books in your genre. Submit a cover letter and a book proposal to various publishers. Your cover letter should contain a summary of your book's ideas, a list of books similar to yours and the reasons your book is different, an explanation of who you are trying to reach, and a sample chapter from your book. Keep trying and do not allow rejection to affect you personally.

Publishers are in the business of publishing books to make money. Since there are so many books being printed, publishers are finding it much harder to create best sellers. They rarely take a

chance on a new author. Do not let this discourage you because it has never been easier for you to publish on your own.

2. Self-Publishing. For a new author, the best solution is to self-publish. For less than a thousand dollars, you can make your book available to the world. With some printing companies, you can print as few as twenty-five copies of your book. As you print more, the cost per unit goes down. For recommendations on which printer to use, call our office and we will provide a list of good printing options.

3. Print-on-Demand. Modern print-on-demand technology is the greatest advancement in book printing since Guttenberg's printing press. When someone orders one of my books from Amazon.com, the book is not even printed until it is paid for. The moment the order is placed, they print my book and mail it out within twenty-four hours. The brilliance of this system is that I do not have to keep thousands of dollars worth of inventory in my garage or in a warehouse; everything happens automatically.

4. An E-Book is a book on a computer. There is no printing cost, no shipping, no mailing, no waiting to get the book. Your reader downloads your book to his computer, mobile device, or e-reader, and you receive instant cash. You might wish to release your book as an e-book first in order to raise money to release it in print later.

5. Audio books. You read the book and record it on CD or release it as an audio download.

Chapter 8

Market Your Book

Once your book is published, you need to move your book off the printing presses and into the hands of people. The masses are now waiting to read your inspired new release! But in order for people to read your book, they need to know it exists and where they can purchase it.

There are a variety of ways for you to market and sell your books. Authors, not the publishers, do the majority of marketing these days. Over 50,000 books will be published this year in America. Only about 5% will be on the shelves of your local bookstore. At first, the majority of your books will be sold to people you know. Here are a few key strategies to expand your buyer base and increase sales.

1. Begin by selling your book to your friends and family. Ask them to buy extra copies to give to their friends. Ask everyone you know to promote the book to their circle of influence.

2. Send out press releases. Our ministry hired someone to send out press releases for my books. These resulted in dozens of radio and television interviews.

3. Use social media. Use Facebook and Twitter to talk about your book. Start a blog. Put up a video on YouTube about your book.

Become known online as an expert in your subject area. As you create buzz online, you will start to sell more books.

4. Give away your book for free. Over 100,000 copies of my book *Welcome to the Kingdom* are in print. We give it away to people who get saved in our overseas services. I frequently send my books free of charge to pastors and ministers. As a minister, I love sowing my books into people's lives. The amazing thing is that the more books I give away, the more I sell.

5. Speak at churches and Bible studies. When you speak on your book topic, audience members will frequently purchase your book. For more information, check out my book *How to Book Speaking Engagements at Churches*.

6. Do a book signing. Ask your local bookstore if you can hold a book signing. Use this as an opportunity to invite everyone you know to come see you at the bookstore. Make it an event.

Conclusion

If God has placed a burning message in your heart, I encourage you to write a book. Your pen can heal someone's pain. Your words can inspire a sinner to follow God. Your book could change the world forever.

Allow your mess to become a message. Turn your tests into a written testimony. As Mike Smalley says, "Allow your pain to become your pulpit." God brought you through the fire, so you can be on fire for Him. Your discoveries and experiences will impact the lives of people you may never meet. As you write, God will use your words to transform eternity.

So what are you waiting for? Grab a pen and paper and start writing. Do not delay, start your book today!

Our Goal?
Every Soul!

Daniel & Jessica King

About the Author

Daniel King and his wife Jessica met in the middle of Africa while they were both on a mission trip. They are in high demand as speakers at churches and conferences all over North America. Their passion, energy, and enthusiasm are enjoyed by audiences everywhere they go.

They are international missionary evangelists who do massive soul-winning festivals in countries around the world. Their passion for the lost has taken them to over fifty nations preaching the gospel to crowds that often exceed 50,000 people.

Daniel was called into the ministry when he was five years old and began to preach when he was six. His parents became missionaries to Mexico when he was ten. When he was fourteen he started a children's ministry that gave him the opportunity to minister in some of America's largest churches while still a teenager.

At the age of fifteen, Daniel read a book where the author encouraged young people to set a goal to earn $1,000,000. Daniel reinterpreted the message and determined to win 1,000,000 people to Christ every year.

Daniel has authored thirteen books including his best sellers *Healing Power*, *The Secret of Obed-Edom*, and *Fire Power*. His book *Welcome to the Kingdom* has been given away to tens of thousands of new believers.

Soul Winning Festivals

Metu, Ethiopia

Khushpur, Pakistan

Roca Blanca, Mexico

Sialkot, Pakistan

Agere Maryam, Ethiopia

Kisaran, Indonesia

Soul Winning Festivals

Dominican Republic

Honduras

Panama

Mexico

Guatemala

Sudan

When Daniel King was fifteen years old, he set a goal to lead 1,000,000 people to Jesus before his 30th birthday. Instead of trying to become a millionaire, he decided to lead a million "heirs" into the kingdom of God. *"If you belong to Christ then you are heirs"* (Galatians 3:29).

After celebrating the completion of this goal, Daniel & Jessica made it their mission to go for one million souls every year.

This **Quest for Souls** is accomplished through:
* Soul Winning Festivals
* Leadership Training
* Literature Distribution
* Humanitarian Relief

Would you help us lead
people to Jesus by joining
The MillionHeir's Club?

Visit www.kingministries.com to get involved!

THE SECRET OF OBED-EDOM

Unlock the secret to supernatural promotion and a more intimate walk with God. Unleash amazing blessing in your life!

$20.00

MOVE

What is God's will for your life? Learn how to find and fulfill your destiny.

$10.00

POWER OF FASTING

Discover deeper intimacy with God and unleash the answer to your prayers.

$10.00

KING MINISTRIES INTERNATIONAL

TOLL FREE: 1-877-431-4276
PO BOX 701113
TULSA, OK 74170 USA

ORDER ONLINE:
WWW.KINGMINISTRIES.COM

MASTER SOUL WINNER

Learn practical tips on sharing your
faith with friends and family.

$10.00

SOUL WINNING

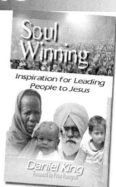

Do you have a passion for the
lost? This book shares over 150
truths about soul winning.

$10.00

WELCOME TO THE KINGDOM

This is a perfect book for new
believers. Learn how to be saved,
healed, and delivered.(Available in
bulk discounts)

$10.00

KING MINISTRIES
INTERNATIONAL

TOLL FREE: 1-877-431-4276
PO BOX 701113
TULSA, OK 74170 USA

ORDER ONLINE:
WWW.KINGMINISTRIES.COM

HEALING POWER

Do you need healing? This power-packed book contains 17 truths to activating your healing today!

$20.00

FIRE POWER

Inside these pages you will learn how to CATCH the fire of God, KEEP the fire of God, and SPREAD the fire of God!

$12.00

POWER OF THE SEED

Discover the power of Seedtime & Harvest! Discover why your giving is the most important thing you will ever do!

$20.00